My Journey with Destiny

By Debra Demi

Dear Readers,

This is the story of my journey with one of the most precious gifts I've ever been given.

In 2006, 22 weeks into my 8th pregnancy, an ultrasound revealed that our unborn baby had a condition called holoprosencephaly - her brain did not divide into 2 hemispheres correctly. We were given the prognosis that she would most likely not be born alive.

This "book" is my spiritual journey during this tumultuous season. It is raw and real. It was not easy. My hope is that you can see how God was with us, and that He will be with you too no matter what you walk through.

One of the ways the Lord cared for me was by providing me with so many good resources. In one way, this is a compilation of what I found to be the most helpful quotes and thoughts from many good books, articles, and podcasts. And most of all, I'm thankful for the Word of God that brought me comfort like no other resource. These snippets are probably the best thing about this journal - so please don't skip over them :-).

Destiny was indeed a precious gift, and so were the lessons He taught us about Himself.

To God be the Glory!
Debbie

Before She Was Born

For you formed my inward parts; you knitted me together in my mother's womb. I praise you, for I am fearfully and wonderfully made. Wonderful are your works; my soul knows it very well. My frame was not hidden from you, when I was being made in secret intricately woven in the depths of the earth. Ps. 139:13 - 15

"In agony and deep affliction, He died that we could enter in. Who can grasp this tender compassion? Who can fathom the depth of His love?"
~I Stand In Awe by Sovereign Grace Music

When I contemplate the agony that Jesus went through on my behalf, how can I doubt His loving-kindness toward me? How can I believe that He's not in control – even of this pregnancy?

April
April 18, 2006 (Tuesday @ 7:11 am)

The ultrasound is starting to weigh on me. Tomorrow is the day! I think that it'll be hard to be pregnant and deal with the uncomfortableness of it all if I know that there is something irreversibly wrong with the baby. I just have to keep going back to the fact that God is in control… that He is a loving God… that He knows what is best for us…

[The ultrasound revealed that the baby has holoprosencephaly and is not expected to make it full term or will die at birth]
April 22, 2006 (Saturday @ 3:33 p.m.)

From Nancy Leigh DeMoss' radio broadcast:

3

"But God is in charge. God knows the timing. *God is in charge.* God has *orchestrated* the timing. 'In the fullness of time,' God brings about His purposes. God picks the time that looks the darkest and seems the most hopeless to show His power and His glory.

But it's an evidence that God has been orchestrating this, because God's grace always shines the most brightly against the darkest backdrop.

God controls all things. Things happen for a reason. We may never know what that reason is, but because God is God we can believe that there is a reason.

If there is no providence, then we have every reason to be terrified because this whole world is chance and out of control, and we ought to be scared to death. But if there is a God who is the creator, who is wise enough and smart enough and loving enough and good enough and able to control every aspect, item, atom, event of his creation, then why would I fear?

So I think when we do fear it's an evidence of the fact that we're not trusting that God is sovereign. We either don't know it, or we don't believe it, or we have forgotten it. But fear cannot coexist with faith. Faith eradicates fear, and faith is based not on some feeling I have but on the reality of who God is and His promises, His character, His sovereignty.

Now does that mean if we're trusting God's sovereignty and providence that there will never be any fear . . . we can just march into the king and feel bold and not have any apprehension about doing that? I think Esther probably did have apprehension, but only to the extent that she didn't know what God was going to do. So any apprehension we do have. . . If we knew what God knows, there would be no fear.

If we really knew God and knew what He was going to do, the more we know about God the less fear there will be. So the less we know about Him, the more we fear, the more we waver, the more. . .

But the more you grow, the more you know, the more you trust . . . as we read in Psalm 9:10, 'Those who know your name will put their trust in you, for you, O LORD, have not forsaken those who seek you.'

The way I used to counsel my heart was to say, 'You know what? It doesn't matter if I come out alive. It doesn't matter if I survive this. What does matter is that I'm doing what God's called me to do. I will go by faith and by God's grace, and in His strength God will give me courage. I will encourage my heart in the Lord. That's to take courage in God. And by God's grace, I will do this.'"

April 24, 2006 (Monday @ 7:19 am)

We're getting ready to walk through the most difficult time of our lives. Today I woke up feeling like a ton of bricks was upon me. The sorrow is so heavy. The cloud above me is so dark. Even though I know the truth – that God is Sovereign, that God is God, that God is loving, that God works all things for my good, that God does not make mistakes, that God will give me the strength to endure… it still hurts so bad. Will every day for the next 3 months feel this way?

I need to embrace this trial and press on. I need to take each step with the burden and feel my faith strengthen. I need to embrace what God has allowed out of His goodness and love and trust God to do a good work out of it. I need God's help to endure

Fenelon – Embracing the Cross
"Endure the aches and pains of your body with patience. Do the same thing with your spiritual afflictions (that is, trouble sent to you that you cannot
control…) Do not resist what God brings into your life. Be willing to suffer if that is what is needed."

"God prepares a cross for you that you must embrace without the thought of self-preservation. The cross is painful. Accept the cross and you will find and you will find peace even in the middle of turmoil."

"See God's hand in the circumstances of your life... Nothing so shortens and soothes your pain as the spirit of non-resistance to your Lord."

"The hardest thing about suffering is not knowing how great it will be or how long it will last. Do not reject the full work that the power of the cross could accomplish in you."

"God loves a cheerful giver. Imagine how much He must love those who abandon themselves to His will cheerfully and completely – even if it results in their crucifixion!"

Matt. 14
Then Peter got down out of the boat, walked on the water and came toward Jesus. [30] But when he saw the wind, he was afraid and, beginning to sink, cried out, "Lord, save me!" [31] Immediately Jesus reached out his hand and caught him. "You of little faith," he said, "why did you doubt?"

Jesus could be saying that to me when I starting sinking into despair, "Why did you doubt?" He's in control!

12:54 pm
The pain is almost unbearable today. It's like I'm carrying a heavy weight over top of my whole body. I keep moving, but the weight is always with
me making each step difficult. The normal tasks of life seem so challenging. I'm set into despair by the simplest of difficulties. I don't even know if each day is going to get easier or harder. There are so many unknowns. I want to walk through this well – yet this big cloud envelops every part of me. Help me, Lord!

April 25, 2006 (Tuesday @ 7:11 am)

I can't believe that it's still April. The month has gone on for so long! I woke up today feeling pretty good, and I do remember thanking the Lord for something as I woke.

Fenelon – Surrender to His Plans

"Will you resist [trials]? No! Allow everything! Volunteer for your own death, for God will only accomplish His work to the extent that you let Him. Do not push away the progress that God wants to make in your life."

"What do your fear, you of little faith? Are you afraid that He may not be able to give you His strength when He takes away yours? Why does He take it away? Only so that He might be your supply."

"Surrender to His plans. Allow yourself to be led where He wants to take you."

All Things for Good – Thomas Watson

- *The evil of temptation is overruled for good to the godly.*
- Satan tempts in subtle ways according to temperament and constitution at the fittest time.
- God can overrule these temptations in the following ways:
    - Temptation sends the soul to prayer.
    - Temptation to sin is a means to keep from the perpetration of sin.
    - Temptation works for good, as it abates the swelling of pride.
    - Temptation works for good, as it is a touchstone to try what is in the heart.
    - Temptations work for good, as God makes those who are tempted, fit to comfort others in the same distress.

April 26, 2006 (Wednesday @ 7:11 am)

Yesterday it seemed like the cloud rolled away for a little while. At times I almost felt like I was either hardened to the situation or denying that there was anything wrong. Sometimes I can feel so sure that there's nothing wrong with the baby. She is so active and kicks so hard. Last night, however, all I could think of was kissing her deformed face and loving this little treasure that God has placed inside of me. I was treasuring each move that she made – knowing that I may never see her move outside of my womb. Those thoughts made me sad. It made me want to pray harder and harder for a miracle. I don't want her to die.

Sometimes I can look past this whole thing and see life "normal" on the other side. The longing will probably always be there for another little girl though.

Fenelon – The Benefit of Trials
"You have some difficult trials to bear but you need them since God has allowed these events to happen. He knows how to select them."

"Sometimes the cross can neither be carried nor dragged. Then you can only fall down beneath it, overwhelmed and exhausted."

"Remember that God is not unaware of your suffering. He allows your suffering. See that He alone knows what is best for you… Confidently trust in God, even when you do not see what He is doing. Trust that God, with great compassion, gives you trials in proportion to the help that He wants to bring to you."

April 27, 2006 (Thursday @ 7:10 am)

It's COMPASS (Homeschool Co-op) day, and I need to get there early for prayer. Each day I just go on and each day happens regardless of my circumstances. I think that I feel less discouraged these days than in the days before the trial.

I've been so tired at night partly because in a way I ignore the fact that I'm pregnant. I don't let myself have the luxury of comfort miseries. I just press on as if I weren't pregnant – like I don't deserve to get the "benefits" of pregnancy.

Judges 7
2 The LORD said to Gideon, "You have too many men for me to deliver Midian into their hands. In order that Israel may not boast against me that her own strength has saved her.

Psalm 70:5 Yet I am poor and needy; come quickly to me, O God. You are my help and my deliverer; O LORD, do not delay.

--- --- --- --- --- --- --- --- --- --- --- --- --- --- --- ---

April 28, 2006 (Friday @ 7:18 am)

I had a really rocky night of sleep last night. I didn't have anything on my mind – I just couldn't sleep. Now I feel really tired and want to climb right back in bed – but I have so much to do today. I just need to keep going!

Fenelon – Trust Your Self-Love to God
"I have no doubt that God treats you as one of his friends by giving you the cross."

May

May 1, 2006 (Monday @ 7:11 am)

Waking up is so hard to do. Every day I want to stay in bed. I can't believe that I'm still getting up!

One of these days I want to sit and write about what I'm going through – the lessons learned, the way that I've changed, the hope and then the hopelessness that I feel. I feel a little better each day, but there's always a weight on me making living a little harder than normal. The pregnancy part is getting harder and harder. I'm getting more and more uncomfortable with respect to just moving and with heartburn, etc. Three more long months to go.

Fenelon – Difficult Circumstances

"Embrace the difficult circumstances you find yourself in – even when you feel they will overwhelm you. Allow God to mold you through the events He allows to enter your life."

"Everything that comes from God's hand produces good fruit. Use the circumstances of each moment to the fullest."

May 2, 2006 (Tuesday @ 7:18 am)

Yesterday was another hard day – not like those beginning days – but full of sadness at times. At B.J.s I had to walk by diapers, Sippy cups, and baby clothes. I was surprised by the emotions that they conjured up. I was not going to be buying any of those things – unless the Lord chooses to heal our little one. She is so active and strong. It's hard to believe that she's not healthy. Karis got to feel her move yesterday. She was thrilled. Then last night I had a dream that she was born – not perfectly healthy, but alive and smart – no clefts or facial deformity. She was weak but could talk. My dreams have become consumed with the future of this baby. How am I going to make it? I'm losing vision for a greater purpose in all of this – it's getting harder and harder. Help me, Lord!

Fenelon – Temper Your Standards
"Suffering is necessary for all of us. You will be purified by dying to your own desires and will. Let yourself die! You have excellent opportunities for this to happen – don't waste them!"

Revive Our Hearts May 2, 2006 (Trusting God)
(Nancy Leigh DeMoss is talking…)
"I've learned a lot about the beauty of a surrendered, submissive heart by some of Elisabeth Elliot's writings. Let me read to you from her

book, _Keep a Quiet Heart_ what she has to say about this whole matter of complaining versus submission.

She says, 'Everything about which we are tempted to complain may be the very instrument whereby the Potter intends to shape His clay into the image of His Son.' The things about which we're tempted to complain may be the very answer to our prayer to be made like Jesus.

Then she lists what some of those may be: 'A headache, an insult, a long line at the checkout, someone's rudeness or failure. to say thank you, misunderstanding, disappointment, interruption. As Amy Carmichael said (I'm quoting Elisabeth Elliot still), 'See in it a chance to die,' meaning a chance to leave self behind and say yes to the will of God, to be conformable unto His death. Not a morbid, martyr complex, but a peaceful and happy contentment in the assurance that goodness and mercy follow us all the days of our lives.'"

_____

May 4, 2006 (Thursday @ 7:16 am)

Sometimes I feel that if I can just get through each day, I'll be alright. Each day has some bright moments and some heavy ones – not much different than my life before BBN (Bad Baby News). When I do get depressed, I find myself evaluating whether it's because of the BBN or just because that is how I've always been. It's amazing how easily I got down before about basically nothing. I think that I get discouraged less now – because I really know how insignificant some of my trials were.

Here's some hard-hitting stuff from Thomas Watson in his book, <u>All Things for Good</u>:
"Learn how little cause we have then to be discontented at outward trials and emergencies! What! Discontented at that which shall do you good! All things shall work for good. There are no sins God's people are more subject to than unbelief and impatience. They are ready either to faint through unbelief or to fret through impatience. When men fly out against God by discontent and impatience it is a sign they do not believe this text. Discontent is an ungrateful sin, because we have more mercies than afflictions; and it is an irrational sin, because afflictions work for good. Discontent is a sin which puts us upon sin. 'Fret not

thyself to do evil' (Psalm 37:8). He that frets will be ready to do evil: fretting Jonah was sinning Jonah. The devil blows the coals of passion and discontent and then warms himself at the fire. Oh, let us not nourish this angry viper in our breast. Let this text produce patience, 'All things work together for good to them that love God' (Rom. 8:28). Shall we be discontented at that which works for our good? If one friend should throw a bag of money at another, and in throwing it, should graze his head, he would not be troubled much, seeing by this means he had got a bag of money. So the Lord may bruise us by afflictions, but it is to enrich us. These afflictions work for us a weight of glory, and shall we be discontented?" pp. 61 – 62

May 5, 2006 (Friday @ 7:18 am)

I actually woke up today feeling happy. Of course in my dreams last night – the baby was born 100% healthy with a thick red hair and smiling. I also led a couple people to the Lord through some kind of book club (a really weird dream). How could you not wake up happy after those 2 dreams?

Romans 5
[3]Not only so, but we also rejoice in our sufferings, because we know that suffering produces perseverance; [4] perseverance, character; and character, hope. [5]And hope does not disappoint us, because God has poured out his love into our hearts by the Holy Spirit, whom he has given us.

God of All Comfort
Chapter 3

"If we want to be comforted, we must make up our minds to believe every single solitary word of comfort God has ever spoken; and we must refuse utterly to listen to any words of discomfort spoken by our own hearts, or by our circumstances. We must set our faces like a flint to believe, under each and every sorrow and trial, in the divine Comforter, and to accept and rejoice in His all-embracing comfort. I say, 'set our faces like a flint,' because, when everything around us seems out of sorts, it is not always easy to believe God's words of comfort. We must put our wills into this matter of being comforted, just as we have to put our wills into all other matters in our spiritual life. We must choose to be comforted."

--- -- --- -- --- -- --- -- --- -- --- -- --- -- --- -- --- -- --- -- --- -- --- -- --- -- --- -- --- -- --- --

May 9, 2006 (Tuesday @ 7:11 am)

I'm getting increasingly more uncomfortable as each day passes. I don't know if it's harder to bear because there isn't the expected joy at the end or if this is how I would feel anyway. I get frustrated because there is so much to do and so much that I want to do – but can't do. Everything is so uncomfortable.

I can be in such a good place with respect to glorifying God in the midst of the trial – only wanting His glory – yet my physical self is struggling so much just to do the dailies. My mind tells me one thing – my body another.

Fenelon – The Hidden Cross
"God has all sorts of circumstances to bring you the cross, and they all accomplish His purpose. He may even join physical weakness to your emotional and spiritual suffering." [Just what I was saying]

The Nature of Self-Denial
"Self-denial consists of bearing patiently all those things that God allows to pass into your life."

"God gives you grace to bear the cross in your life just like He provides for your daily bread. He will never fail you!"

The God of All Comfort
Chapter 7
"Goodness in Him must mean, just as it does with us, the living up to the best and highest He knows.

Practically, then, it means that He will not neglect any of His duties toward us and that He will always treat us in the best possible way."

"If our faith were what it ought to be, no circumstances, however untoward, could make us 'limit' the power of God to supply our needs. The God who can make circumstances can surely control circumstances, and can, even in the wilderness, 'furnish a table' for all who trust in Him."

May 11, 2006 (Thursday @ 7:13 am)

I cried 3 nights in a row. Today I woke up with a heavy cloud on me. Reality has hit again. Sometimes I just carry on as if the baby is fine and that all is going to work out. I keep praying that God would heal the baby and totally believe that he can. When she's so active in there, I have such a hard time believing that there's anything wrong with her. It's so easy to lose my focus – that God's in control and knows how to measure my trials perfectly. Pregnancy mixed with life mixed with death is so hard.

Romans 12 - 13
[12] Be joyful in hope, patient in affliction, faithful in prayer. [13] Share with God's people who are in need. Practice hospitality.
The God of All Comfort
Chapter 15
"And could we but see, in our heaviest trials, the end from the beginning, I am sure that thanksgiving would take the place of complaining in every case."

May 15, 2006 (Monday @ 7:15 am)

Monday mornings are so hard to do!

So many lessons to be learned from this trial… One way that it has affected me is that I'm trying to apply that sense of God's goodness and control that I'm feeling with respect to the baby, to our other kids' behavior. I feel like God's not really in control in their lives and that it's up to us to fix them. When I have a little bit of control over a circumstance, I have trouble letting it go and letting God do the work – in resting in God. My take-home point is that God is even in control of them and instead of worrying and striving, I need to rest and pray.

Ephesians

1:11 In him we were also chosen, having been predestined according to the plan <u>of him who works out everything in conformity with the purpose of his will,</u> [12]in order that we, who were the first to hope in Christ, might be for the praise of his glory.

The same power that raised Christ from the dead is working in us daily! How do we access this power or do we need to?

Ephesians 4:1 As a prisoner for the Lord, then, I urge you to live a life worthy of the calling you have received.

May 24, 2006 (Wednesday @ 7:13 am)

My quiet times have been nothing more than a habit, and I dread walking on the treadmill. I need a revival spiritually – again. I can't believe how bad I feel with this pregnancy and I still have 2+ months to go. This is so hard. Help me, Lord! Heal this little one that you have created!

June

June 15, 2006 (Thursday @ 7:39 am)

Somehow I totally slipped out of the quiet time habit. Getting up has been so difficult for me – life, in general, has been so difficult. I don't know if it's just the pregnancy or the complications of pregnancy (the diagnosis) that has made it so difficult or if it's just laziness. I feel myself slipping into despair and don't know how to get out – except through meeting with the Lord – which I am fighting against.

June 16, 2006 (Friday @ 7:20 am)

Things are getting more and more difficult with this pregnancy and I'm seriously losing perspective. I'm having trouble finishing the race well. We're going to have another ultrasound at CHOP probably next week for a more thorough diagnosis. I failed my glucose test and need to take the 3-hour test next week as well. I knew that I was going to fail and probably do have gestational diabetes which equals more doctors visits and tests. I don't feel like doing anything (but Sudoku puzzles), but somehow or other I keep pressing on. A little over 7 weeks to go. I'm floundering and don't know what to do. I keep crying out to God to help me and I'm expectantly waiting to hear from Him. I'm back to the crying thing – just about every time I go into the bathroom I have an outbreak. This, so far, has definitely been the worse time of my entire life. I want to live for God's glory in the midst of it, but my inner turmoil is so great!

Colossians
My joy (according to Colossians) should be based solely on my salvation – being rescued from the kingdom of darkness. No trial should be able to usurp that joy. I'm having trouble getting there.

"Continue to live in Him… overflowing with thankfulness." Col. 2:6

June 19, 2006 (Monday @ 7:25 am)

Sleeping has been rather difficult for me due to the heat. The house stays cold except for our bedroom – I don't know what's up with that? I was up and down last night... I need to schedule my blood sugar test today. I know that I'm going to fail – I feel like my blood sugar is high. The heat makes me so sluggish. I wonder how I would feel if I knew that the baby was going to be o.k.?

Next week we'll be going to CHOP for some major testing on the baby. I'm praying for God to heal her completely, yet trying not to base all my confidence for grace on that. I'm losing my vision for what God has for us in this trial; that total trust in His will and the desire to deny myself and glorify Him completely is waning. The uncomfortableness of the pregnancy coupled with the big day drawing near – seems to be pushing any joy that I could have away. Soon we'll see our little Destiny Hope – and I'm dreading the day.

Psalm 78

21 When the LORD heard them, he was very angry; his fire broke out against Jacob, and his wrath rose against Israel, 22 for they did not believe in God or trust in his deliverance.

I find myself in this place – not believing in God or trusting in his deliverance for my circumstances! God is not pleased with this – He wants our total trust even when we can't see any possible good coming from our circumstances!

June 20, 2006 (Tuesday @ 7:41 am)

It seems like just about anything that could go wrong with this pregnancy has gone wrong. I feel like I'm living a nightmare. There are so many good things going on – the other kids are healthy, our house is great, church is good, and our marriage is thriving. But it's so hard to get away from the effects of this pregnancy. I feel like I'm constantly running to catch up with something, but just miss grabbing on to it. Last week was crazy with all of the test results (CHOP, blood sugar, insurance issues) along with Father's Day, Josh's birthday and portfolios. I don't feel like I'm going to make it, but what else is there to do? The way life moves, you just have to make it.

With all of the insurance junk going on yesterday, I found myself wondering what God was doing. Why does this have to happen too? In my head, I was saying, "Give us a break, God!" I want to believe with all of my heart that God is in control and has a good purpose for all of this. Yet it's so hard to see! It looks like we'll save some money because of this insurance deal. I'm going to skip my blood sugar tests (much to the chagrin of the midwives I'm sure). We won't get to go to CHOP for a couple of weeks – which who knows, God may heal in that time. The stress, however, keeps building. I'm not sure what to do – when hope is gone. Only He can sustain me. Last night I felt a little like how I felt when we were selling our house – wanting to fully trust God and wanting to dig in the pit of self-pity and despair. I remembered how I failed at that time – which actually gave me hope to trust this time. Didn't God take care of all the house details in a way that I couldn't have imagined (all for our good)? Why then can't I believe that He's working through the insurance, blood sugar, CHOP, pregnancy issues as well?

I want to blame all my "down" feelings on this pregnancy – but the reality is that I've always had these kinds of days where I don't feel like going on. This trial is revealing to me that there is something deeper going on when I feel down when there's nothing wrong. I need to analyze why that is. I still want to squeeze out every ounce of good from this trial and learn what God has to teach me!

June 21, 2006 (Wednesday @ 7:41 am)

Jonah 2:8
  "Those who cling to worthless idols
      forfeit the grace that could be theirs."

This is an interesting verse. When we hold onto things that replace God in our lives we forfeit grace.

June 23, 2006 (Friday @ 7:55 am)

The dark cloud of my circumstances again is heavy upon me. The weight seems more than I can bear – yet I am still bearing and pressing on – only by God's sustaining grace. I can't wait for this nightmare to end – the pain to cease… life to be "normal" if it can ever be normal for me. Oh God, rescue me; bring back my joy!

Psalm 86
4 Bring joy to your servant,
    for to you, O Lord,
    I lift up my soul.
5 You are forgiving and good, O Lord,
    abounding in love to all who call to you.
6 Hear my prayer, O LORD;
    listen to my cry for mercy.
7 In the day of my trouble I will call to you,
    for you will answer me.

June 26, 2006 (Monday @ 7:45 am)

There's so much to do in the morning – quiet time, exercise/prayer and shower/get ready that I don't get downstairs until after 9 – even when I do get up at 7:00.

The Merry-Go-Round ride continues! It sometimes spins so fast that I can't see straight. My son Luke's Bolivia trip was postponed due to a plane delay. It made yesterday kind of crazy! I think that I'm starting to get used to being pregnant. I've come to enjoy her little kicks and squirms – I just wish she was healthy. At times I forget about all the details… insurance issues and pregnancy complications; at other times I'm completely overwhelmed and emotional.

June 28, 2006 (Wednesday @ 7:44 am)

Wow, June has flown by. Only 1 more month of being pregnant. These last few weeks have not been bad physically.

Psalm 90:12 Teach us to number our days aright, that we may gain a heart of wisdom.

June 29, 2006 (Thursday @ 7:40 am)

Yesterday, I actually felt pretty up – probably because I got a lot accomplished in my organizing the house and typing up objectives. The baby thing is getting scarier and scarier as I seriously contemplate bringing home the baby without her being healed. In my mind, I picture her being completely healthy. I'm feeling God's grace though.

Psalm 91
1 He who dwells in the shelter of the Most High will rest in the shadow of the Almighty.

We need to dwell in the Lord's shelter, that we may rest in his shadow!

Luke 1
38"I am the Lord's servant," Mary answered. "May it be to me as you have said." Then the angel left her.

May I say this about the child that the Lord has placed in my womb!

June 30, 2006 (Friday @ 7:41 am)

The last day of June. D-day is coming around so quickly at this point. It doesn't feel the same as the other babies. I'm not in a big rush to end this pregnancy. I feel pretty good and am getting used to carrying around this extra weight with all of her squirming. It's sad to think of what d-day will bring – the end of a life or the beginning of another trial. I know that God has ordained all of this and will give us the grace to carry on. I continue to pray that the baby is healed. I can't even imagine the joy of adding another healthy child to our family – a baby girl no less. Bless us, Lord, I pray!

July

July 3, 2006

July 5, 2006 (Wednesday @ 3:22 pm)

I'm coming to the end of this current race – this pregnancy. It doesn't seem to be a matter of finishing quickly whatsoever, but of finishing faithfully with my eyes on the goal. Anyway, I've never really put my thoughts and experiences – the things that the Lord has taught me into words. I have little snippets of thoughts throughout the last 3 months, but no point-by-point lessons. So here it goes…

Randomly…
+ God has allowed this trial and therefore has measured it perfectly for my good and his glory.
"Remember that God is not unaware of your suffering. He allows your suffering. See that He alone knows what is best for you… Confidently trust in God, even when you do not see what He is doing. Trust that God, with great compassion, gives you trials in proportion to the help that He wants to bring to you." Fenelon

+ I don't want to waste my suffering. It's not a time to soak into myself – but to see what God has for me in the midst of this time. Who does he want me to share with? How can I encourage others with the encouragement that I've received from the Lord? How does God want to work in my heart?
Here's some hard-hitting stuff from Thomas Watson in his book, "All Things for Good" …
"Will you resist [trials]? No! Allow everything! Volunteer for your own death, for God will only accomplish His work to the extent that

21

you let Him. Do not push away the progress that God wants to make in your life."

"What do your fear, you of little faith? Are you afraid that He may not be able to give you His strength when He takes away yours? Why does He take it away? Only so that He might be your supply."

"Surrender to His plans. Allow yourself to be led where He wants to take you. Be careful when you seek help from people when God is not wanting you to." Fenelon

+ **My mind needs to dictate my emotions. I need to dwell on what I know is true of God. I need to be thankful for what I do have. I have 7 healthy kids! I have a good marriage, a nice house, my health... the list of things to be thankful for goes on and on. How could I ever say, "Why me?"**

"If we want to be comforted, we must make up our minds to believe every single solitary word of comfort God has ever spoken; and we must refuse utterly to listen to any words of discomfort spoken by our own hearts, or by our circumstances. We must set our faces like a flint to believe, under each and every sorrow and trial, in the divine Comforter, and to accept and rejoice in His all-embracing comfort. I say, "set our faces like a flint," because, when everything around us seems out of sorts, it is not always easy to believe God's words of comfort. We must put our wills into this matter of being comforted, just as we have to put our wills into all other matters in our spiritual life. We must choose to be comforted." Smith

+ **This is an opportunity to trust God. I always see his purposes after the fact. We couldn't sell our house because this house wasn't available yet. However, I couldn't see that or trust God in that at the time – even though I should have been able to (what a small trial). The insurance issue weighed heavily on me – yet I should have been able to see that God had a purpose in delaying that as well. My blood sugar was high (= stress), yet now because of the diet, I feel and sleep so much better. Who knows what God is working through this baby. It may just be in all the transformations within me, the work that is occurring in our marriage, things in my life that never surfaced before that have needed to be dealt with. Maybe God will heal the baby and bring many to faith in him. We may never know the reason, but my goal**

needs to be to trust God in the trial and to look for the ways that God is working in the midst of the trial for my good and his glory.

Difficult Circumstances
"Embrace the difficult circumstances you find yourself in – even when you feel they will overwhelm you. Allow God to mold you through the events He allows to enter your life."
"Everything that comes from God's hand produces good fruit. Use the circumstances of each moment to the fullest." Fenelon

+ If I believe that God is in control of this "big" circumstance – it helps me to believe that He is in control of all the "minor" circumstances. Not only is God the God of this baby, He's the God of our finances. Sometimes it's easier to trust God with a big trial than a little irritation.

July 14, 2006 (Friday @ 1:35 pm)

It's been a very rough week. CHOP was intense and brought it all close to the emotional front again.

Here's my life lesson that I need to capture now – even while the chicken sits defrosted and the water boils aimlessly on the stove.

It feels like everything is going wrong all around... the insurance issues, the bad baby news, failing tests, ... It all hurts right now in an emotional way as a surgery to remove a large cancerous tumor would hurt physically. If we didn't know what we were being saved from, the surgery would feel like trouble upon trouble... the incision, the bills, the recovery process... Yet, what a benefit the surgery would be: it would keep one from death; it would remove future pain; it would allow one to live life to the fullest. What's going on in our lives at this time could be God's way of doing surgery on our souls – we just can't see what the pain is sparing us from or preparing us to do or how it will be used for the future. It's all a matter of faith in a God who is faithful. A God who doesn't allow pain for the sake of pain – but has a plan even for the pain that seems unnecessary. We just can't see the work that He is inevitably doing beneath the surface. He's allowing circumstances that if we could see the outcome of His plan – we would say, "Cut deeper." May we not miss what He intends!

———————————————————————————————————————

July 16, 2006 (Sunday @ 11:40 pm)

More life lessons… continual life lessons…
Will life ever be easy… especially at 42 on? I don't think so. After this trial, there will be another and another. It may be going through more teenage crisis's, dealing with elderly parents, overcoming various health problems ourselves or watching grown children with their own struggles. Somewhere in life, I need to be able to enjoy life in the midst of a crisis because there will probably always be one in various degrees. I need to be content without constant amazements and accolades. How I overcome, however, I don't know.

Going through this trial I've come face to face with my many weaknesses. Those alone have caused me to fall into repeated despair. I see my sins in my kids, yet I keep sinning. My kids fail, and I take it on personally. Life is crashing in around me on all sides, and I'm clueless as to how to overcome.

———————————————————————————————————————

July 31, 2006 (Monday @ 7:57 am)

It's been a while since I've had an official quiet time. I feel justified for some reason at this point in my pregnancy. If I want to soak everything out of this trial for God's glory, I can't be doing it on my own strength.
I have officially 1 week to go before my due date of August 7th. Unlike other pregnancies, I don't have that burning desire to be done being pregnant. I'm getting used to being uncomfortable and content with being big and slow. I'm not looking forward to the day and seeing the new little Demi. Anxiety comes and goes. I need to believe that God has grace for me in whatever the outcome. We have so many people praying for us. It's unbelievable to have so much support. How could I possibly doubt that God has a major plan through this whole ordeal? I don't want to get in His way. I don't want to force anything just to make something happen, yet I need to position myself to be in the best usable condition.

Psalm 91

14 "Because he loves me," says the LORD, "I will rescue him; I will protect him, for he acknowledges my name.

15 He will call upon me, and I will answer him; I will be with him in trouble...

1 Peter 1

[6] In this (salvation) you greatly rejoice, though now for a little while you may have had to suffer grief in all kinds of trials. [7] These have come so that your faith—of greater worth than gold, which perishes even though refined by fire—may be proved genuine and may result in praise, glory, and honor when Jesus Christ is revealed.

It seems like it's been so long since the Word has really spoken to me - that I've taken a scripture from my reading into the day to meditate on. What's wrong with me? Why won't these truths stick?

There have been so many lessons that I've learned through this trial; not just the baby trial but through the whole year of ups and downs with moving and finding jobs.

Probably one of the biggest lessons that I've learned and trying to appropriate and rest in is that God has a plan behind each disappointment and behind his seeming slowness in answering my prayers. I fretted when our house wouldn't sell and when we had all of those complications with the buyers. I fretted when Jeff lost his job at closing. I've seen God do amazing works in his timing. Look where we live? God arranged that! I know that God is working through our children's failures to make them (and us) into the people he wants to use for his glory. I have to rest that God is working through this baby situation. Although it's much harder than the other "trials," He's still at work in probably even a greater way. May I not fret.

Psalm 37:8

Refrain from anger and turn from wrath; do not **fret**—it leads only to evil.

August

Destiny's Short Life (August 8, 2006 - November 4, 2006)

*Your eyes saw my unformed substance; in your book were written,
every one of them, the days that were formed for me, when as yet there
was none of them. Ps. 139:16*

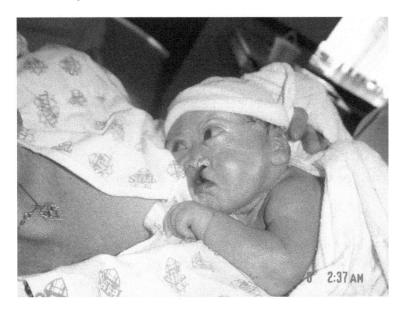

2:37 AM

August 10, 2006 (Thursday @ 10:35 pm)

What a difficult day! Destiny Hope was born into our family on
Tuesday, August 8th @ 2:40 pm. Her birth was a miracle despite all of
her physical and mental handicaps. We were and are still amazed at the
grace that God has bestowed upon us in the midst of this trial. God's
people have been blessing us immensely as well as people who don't
even know us. We feel thoroughly blessed by God in the midst of our
circumstances.

Today was difficult because Destiny's health seems to be
deteriorating. Her breathing was so labored today that I thought that she
was going to suffocate to death. She was having multiple seizures –
non-stop seizures. It was so scary to watch. Then in the midst of her

worst point, Jeff's sister called to say that Jeff's dad had a massive heart attack. It's been extremely emotional and draining. All we can do is trust that God is still good. That He is in control… that His timing is perfect – though we can't see it right now. We pray that God will give us the wisdom to walk through this, to make wise decisions regarding Destiny and traveling to Altoona; that God would heal Jack miraculously.

August 24, 2006 (Thursday @ 12:47 pm)

Destiny is now 2 weeks and 2 days old. Since she's been born life has been a roller coaster. Jeff's dad died last week and we traveled back and forth from Altoona twice. Destiny is doing well for the most part – but has seizures all of the time. I feel so bad for her. The hardest thing has been the middle of the night. She has an awake, crying period from about 12 – 3 a.m. We feel totally helpless and always tired. There always seems to be a big ugly cloud looming overhead. I wouldn't say that life has lost its joy – but something has definitely changed. Everything seems hard and stressful. I keep getting different types of headaches – from sinus headaches to migraines. I feel so weak and vulnerable.

Even though things are really hard right now – there is a definite sense that God is working behind the scenes to accomplish His purposes. We cannot see what He is doing, but He's given us the confidence that He is doing something magnificent through Destiny's life and even through our trust in Him. Many people have commented to us how they admire our faith – yet we trust that God will do more than just have people admire us. We desire much fruit in other people's lives (especially our kids) and for many to come to salvation through Destiny's life and the gift of faith that God has given us. I'm thankful that I can still say that God is good. If He's not good all of the time – then He's not God. May God be glorified through this trial and may we at some point see why God has allowed this. I continue to pray that Destiny would be healed; that the doctors would have wisdom and care for her; that we would have the strength to carry on without our bodies breaking down. Help us, Lord!

Baby Dedication August 20th (Read at Covenant Fellowship Church)

Two weeks ago, we didn't think we would be standing here at this baby dedication because...

We had little hope for our baby Destiny to live. About 4 ½ months ago, 22 weeks into Deb's 8th pregnancy, an ultrasound revealed to us that our baby had a condition called holoprosencephaly. At 6 – 7 weeks, her brain did not divide and therefore, she is basically missing the front of her brain. The doctor gave us the grave news that her condition was fatal (lethal as she called it). She expressed her condolences and said that they would not stop labor if it began early and that they would not do a C-section to save her life.

With 18 weeks remaining in the pregnancy, we began to ponder and embrace the possible outcomes. Would she die at birth or was there a possibility that she would live? If she lived, then how long and what would be her condition? We didn't buy any baby items to help prepare us for her possible death.

Even though the weeks of uncertainty were difficult, we were not alone during this time. Our community group and many others from Covenant Fellowship supported us with continual prayers and much encouragement. Through it all God met us at every turn and gave us peace. Even though it was not always easy, we found that there was no dark corner our minds could go where we did not also find our Savior. We found ourselves grateful that the Lord gave us those 18 weeks to ponder what the Lord was doing in our lives and to grow in love for our unborn baby.

However, 12 days ago Destiny was born alive. The joy we experienced at her birth was unlike any other. Death was looming in our minds and every indicator prior to birth seemed to confirm that Destiny would not survive the birth. However, to us, her birth was miraculous. She was born with the condition that she was diagnosed with. She has a cleft lip, a cleft palate suffers from seizures and multiple other conditions that we have yet to experience. But we are so grateful for the opportunity to have Destiny in our family and to care for her – even if her time on earth is short. She has continued to surprise us with her will to live.

It seems to be Destiny is here just for us. God has packaged up a little life for us to experience more of him. God, the one who can see all things with eternity in view, with infinite love and wisdom, brought Destiny Hope into our family and into this church for reasons we don't yet fully know. We know that our family will be forever changed because of her life.

God has blessed us with seven wonderful children over the years - all of whom we have dedicated to the Lord. But to dedicate Destiny today is special because...

Despite her condition. we know that before the creation of time, God planned Destiny to be born into our family at just this time. He knitted her together in Debbie's womb and she is fearfully and wonderfully made. All her days were ordained and written in His book before one of them came to be. We want to embrace what He has for us through her life. We want to celebrate the fact that God is good all of the time that His ways are perfect even though they don't always look that way from the outside. It's an opportunity to trust God in a way that we've never had to before and to honor Him as we walk through something that He has carefully and lovingly chosen for us to accomplish His good purposes.

We don't know how long we will be blessed to have Destiny with us. Each day is a struggle for her. We are continually crying out to God for wisdom in how to care for her needs. Yet, just like all of our children, we know that she is a blessing from the Lord and we offer her back to Him for His glory.

August 26, 2006 (Saturday @ 11:29 pm)

My heart is in agony and probably will end up there many times through Destiny's life. Jeff just took her to the emergency room to get her seizures evaluated. There's a possibility that they will admit her and keep her. I don't want to be away from her.

Oh, Lord Jesus, I cry out to you to help us. Please bless us with the best doctors and give them much wisdom to care for our sweet little girl. Give Jeff wisdom to make decisions that will serve her best. Help the doctors to help her by eliminating the seizures. Protect her in every way. Give my heart peace. Are we doing the right thing? I can't stop crying. This is so much harder than I ever imagined. How can I love someone so much? I need your grace now Lord – to sleep, to pray, to be at peace, to trust you! Heal our little one. When they look into her brain tonight may they see your complete healing. You are able to heal her. Do a miracle for this little one you have created! I need your peace, Lord.

August 31, 2006 (Thursday @ 7:42 am)

Yesterday I actually had a normal feeling day – despite the many of phone calls on Destiny's behalf. I felt an extraordinary measure of God's grace. The saints were obviously praying.

Fenelon – Live Day by Day
"You really need to believe that God keeps His word. The more you trust Him, the more He will be able to give you. Fear nothing but to fail God. And do not even fear that so much that you let it upset you. Live day by day, not in your own strength, but by completely surrendering to God."

"All Things For Good" (Blog Post from GirlTalk)

2006 at 8:38 am | by Nicole Whitacre

Filed under Biblical Womanhood Suffering

Today we want you to hear--and learn--from Debbie Demi, a member of our sister church, Covenant Fellowship in Philadelphia. "After regeneration, one of the greatest miracles of grace, is the Christian who rejoices in the midst of suffering" my dad has said. This family is truly a miracle of grace. Here is Debbie's answer to our question, "*tell us about a circumstance in your life where you now see God was working 'behind the scenes' for your good?*"

Recently my family has been going through the toughest trial of our lives. Twenty-two weeks into my pregnancy with our eighth child, an ultrasound revealed that our unborn baby girl had a condition called holoprosencephaly. At 6–7 weeks, her brain did not divide and therefore, it was determined that she was missing the front part of her brain. The doctor gave us the grave news that her condition was fatal (lethal as she called it). She expressed her condolences and said that they would not stop labor if it began early and that they would not do a C-section to save her life.

To most onlookers, it appeared that there could not possibly be any good to come from such a diagnosis. In a doctor's report, he called it "an unfortunate pregnancy." However, with eyes of faith and an eternal perspective, God by His grace has allowed us to see that, "He works all things together for our good."

Three weeks ago, Destiny was born alive. The joy we experienced at her birth was unlike any other. Death was looming in our minds and every indicator prior to birth seemed to confirm that Destiny would not survive the birth. Therefore, to us, her birth was miraculous. She was born with the condition that she was diagnosed with. She has a cleft lip, a cleft palate, suffers from seizures and multiple other conditions that we have yet to experience. However, we are so grateful for the opportunity to have Destiny in our family and to care for her – even if her time on earth is short.

Even though the trial is not over, we can by faith believe that God is working for our good and look for ways God is working even in the midst of the most trying times knowing that nothing happens by chance. We don't know the extent of how God is going to use Destiny for our good and His glory, but here are just a couple ways that we've seen him work so far.

1) We believe that He's teaching our children compassion as they care for a handicapped child; growing their faith by allowing them to see us glorifying God in a trial and seeing God answer our prayers; teaching them to care for others as they see the body of Christ caring for us. By faith, knowing the character of God, we know that He is doing an eternal work in their hearts through this trial.

2) As my husband and I have walked through this together, I've grown in love and admiration for my him. I've seen strengths in him that I would never have seen otherwise as I've experienced his care and marveled at the way he has shepherded our family.

3) We've experienced the care from the body of Christ in a way that we never imagined, teaching us how to serve others and bearing testimony of the Gospel to our unsaved family members and neighbors. They will know we are Christians by our love.

4) It's been an opportunity for us not to waste our suffering, but to use every opportunity to glorify God in what He, by His loving hand, has allowed into our lives. God has allowed us to experience Him in a

deeper way, to experience His faithfulness in a difficult situation, to ponder what He has done for us on the cross, to draw closer to Him. How much greater good could we receive than to know Christ our Savior more?

"Let this text produce patience, 'All things work together for good to them that love God' (Rom. 8:28). Shall we be discontented at that which works for our good? If one friend should throw a bag of money at another, and in throwing it, should graze his head, he would not be troubled much, seeing by this means he had got a bag of money. So the Lord may bruise us by afflictions, but it is to enrich us. These afflictions work for us a weight of glory, and shall we be discontented?" *All Things for Good* by Thomas Watson pp. 61 – 62

October

October 19, 2006 (Thursday @ 7:07 am)

I missed the whole month of September. No journaling for that month. It's been totally crazy! I know that this has been the most difficult time of my life. I've never felt so stripped bare and helpless. I'm not able to do what I want to do except in very little pockets of time. I feel pretty weary. However, I did have one insight that came to me yesterday while watching Jake and Josh play football…

I was getting discouraged about my inability to do just about everything… have neighbors over, do things with the kids, do household projects, keep the house clean, make nice meals… I was thinking about the purposelessness of my life. Then, the Holy Spirit filled me and spoke to me. I have an opportunity to be a sweet fragrance to my children through this trial. This is my opportunity to respond to each situation in a way that will teach them about Christ. I don't have much control over my life at this point… especially in how I minister outside of my home. But, what an opportunity to disciple my children in trusting God, in reacting to difficult circumstances (spilling of water, breaking things, arguments – everyday circumstances should I say) – in a way that glorifies and trusts God. I can't see this type of service as insignificant. This responding is my calling right now. I can't be looking for a bigger calling or a more glamorous calling… this is my calling to respond like Christ in my home. What volumes I will be teaching my kids! My life, even as chaotic as it is – has significance in a much bigger way than I ever imagined. Yes, I will fail. I already failed miserably last night – but with God's help, I will point my kids towards Christ especially now that I'm aware of this holy calling.

I'm determined, as there is power within me by God, to capitalize on this difficult time. He has much to teach me during it. I know that He is doing a great work and I want to cooperate in what He is doing and not fight against His plan.

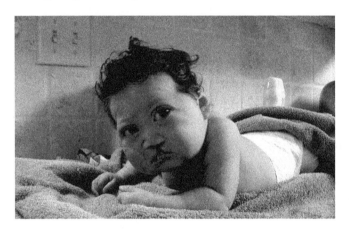

November

November 2, 2006 (Wednesday/Thursday)

Destiny is in the hospital again – aspiration pneumonia is the diagnosis. Her pulse ox is really low. She just doesn't seem to be doing well. I vacillate between wanting to ball my eyes out and resting totally in God's plan. I don't think that crying would necessarily be wrong; it does hurt and it is sad – but it's probably not the best thing to do right now. I feel a pain deep down inside, yet there's this rising up feeling that I have in bearing the pain. It's almost the same feeling that I get when I exercise – it hurts too, yet there is a good feeling somewhere in the pain. There is also an end result of strength from exercising, just as I know that as I persevere through this trial, there will be fruit worthy of the pain.

Back to my thoughts from last week… I was listening to a talk by Nancy Leigh DeMoss on hospitality. A feeling of "I want to do that" mingled with guilt came upon me. Reality struck me too – "This may not be the time for hospitality." Again I heard that still small voice speak, "You at this time are called to respond in a godly way to your children in all circumstances, and in this, I am greatly pleased and you are doing a great work in my eyes." I feel like the Lord has given me a new picture of my purpose in life. It's not to "do, do, do" (things that outwardly are rewarding and seemingly spiritual), but simply "be" a reflection of Christ in my home. Amazingly, I can already see fruit after only one week. It's amazing how much my kids imitate my behavior and how the atmosphere in my home changes with my reactions and responses to what is going on around me. This lesson is just another way that God is using this trial in my life. God is honoring my desire to squeeze every ounce of God out of these difficult circumstances. I am changing, by God's grace, and know that he will continue to work in ways that I could have never asked or imagined. My prayer is that Destiny will bring many to salvation through her life.

I continue to pray that Destiny will be healed. I look for the miracle. However, I am confident that God is in control and has a significant purpose in bringing her into our lives.

Destiny's Death
November 6, 2006 (Monday @ 8:12 am)

Thoughts from Mom,
 (In the program at the funeral)

My dear sweet Destiny died two days ago. It's amazing how much you could love someone who did so little so much. I marveled in anything that she could do. We were excited every time she went "poo poo" on her own or turned her eyes to look at something. Her body was perfect. I marveled at her little toes and fingers and beautiful hair. She was mine, especially designed by God for me for a time such as this, and I loved her.

Destiny was a lot of work. She required medicine to make each part of her work – a medicine to sleep, a medicine not to seize, a medicine to move her bowels, a medicine to help keep food in her stomach… I cried many nights since she was born – saddened by what her future held and fearful of when her last day would come. The doctors and hospital visits were getting exhausting. I felt like I was in the 4th watch (as it says in the bible). I was weary – yet at the same time, I was confident that the Lord would not give me more than I could handle.

I would have never chosen this trial or any trial for that matter. The pain of losing a child is at times unbearable. Yet, by God's grace, I was able to press into God and try to see what purpose He had in bringing Destiny into my life – because I have no doubt that God doesn't allow anything without a specific purpose. He had everything calculated down to the minutest detail including the perfect number of her days to accomplish the purpose that He had in mind for us. He knew the exact amount of pain and emotional energy that I could handle to keep me pressing into Him – that it wouldn't be too much that I would grow weary or bitter. I always knew and still continue to rest on the fact that He is good all of the time and not only is He good – but all things that He allows into our lives are for our good. We can't always see how a circumstance like this could be good – yet our confidence is not in how we feel or how we see things – but in who God is.

We often think that all pain is bad and that it's our goal to avoid it at all costs – It all hurts right now in an emotional way as a surgery to remove a large cancerous tumor would hurt physically. If we didn't know what we were being saved from, the surgery would feel like trouble upon trouble… the incision, the bills, the recovery process… Yet, what a benefit the surgery would be: it would keep one from death; it would remove future pain; it would allow one to live life to the fullest. What's going on in our lives at this time could be God's way of doing surgery on our souls – we just can't see what the pain is sparing us from or preparing us to do or how it will be used for the future. It's all a matter of faith in a God who is faithful. A God who doesn't allow pain for the sake of pain – but has a plan even for the pain that seems unnecessary. We just can't see the work that He is inevitably doing beneath the surface. He's allowing circumstances that if we could see the outcome of His plan – we would say, "Cut deeper." May we not miss what He intends!

Destiny's name means, "for which you were meant to do." She accomplished what her loving Creator meant her to do on earth. Now we have the hope that she will spend eternity with Him in glory where we will be with her one day.

Thoughts from Dad (read at the funeral):

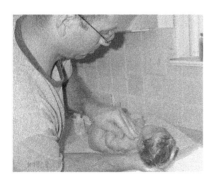

Destiny's life was short and may have seemed from the surface to have not been very significant.

Destiny had so very little.
She never did anything that the world would count as an accomplishment.

She saw dimly at best.
She heard few sounds.
She never learned how to say I love you.
She never went to school, married, or got a job .

But we know a person's life is not measured this way in the eyes of God!

Consider the story Jesus told about the Rich Man and Lazarus
If someone calculated the life of Lazarus on the surface he would most
likely conclude that it was a waste. The rich man's life would have
seemed significant and meaningful.

But God has a different measure. Lazarus was thought of greatly and
after his death angels carried him to Abraham's side; while the rich man
whose name we don't even know, is separated from God, without
anything and in agony wishing that none of his family would follow
him there.

Destiny's life would seem wasteful to the world, but how great she
must have been in the eyes of Jesus.

And when I think about it, I can find no wrong or evil that her life
begot. Her worst thing going for her was her association with me. And
even that has been taken care of. I'm confident that God has taken care
of my worst problems and offenses by the blood of his Son, Jesus.
    In fact, she accomplished many things:

- She won the battle of life or death at birth!
- She did several pushups.
- She rolled over once.
- She endured the pain of multiple IV attempts.
- For the few who got to see it, she smiled real big.
- She crept into the hearts of hundreds.
- She forever changed our perspective on this world.
- Destiny changed our home forever. She really was a gift to us from God.
- With no real hope for this world, she became an instrument of grace to our family.

I'm not trying to minimize the work or struggles it was to care for her at
times but it's those very struggles that God used to work in our lives.

38

- She had numerous following of concerned people and prayer partners.
- She broke into our lives and dispelled what can be a parent's greatest fear.
- She reminded us to love this world less.
- She reminds us of our immortality and that the end of life on this earth can come at any time with no warning.
- She showed us how to love those who would seem to be hard to love.

Daily routine

- Caring for Destiny each day had its challenges.
- When we could feed her no longer, the Lord blessed us with an NG tube.
- When her seizures took over her body, the Lord blessed us with doctors and medicines to control them.
- When exhaustion overtook us, the Lord gave us good sleep.
- Loneliness and fear seldom got very far into our lives. God surrounded us with the unbelievable thoughtfulness and encouragement of his people, friends, and family. We thank God for his promises and his presence that sustained us through every situation

But right now I wouldn't trade one moment that I had with her. They are all treasures stored up for me to enjoy for the rest of my life. Not the all-night hospital stays, or any middle-of-the-night happenings. Not the measuring of medications, the slow feeding or the cleaning up the spit up. I'll remember the baths and the feedings. I treasure the memory of her beautiful eyes and long soft hair.

We thank God for her!
Now Destiny is in heaven with a new body. Now that she is able to express herself fully, here are some of the things that I think she would like to say to those who knew her.

- Thank you, Mom, for talking to me with such a lovely voice, for feeding me such good food, for your happiness around me. I wanted to do something special for you but it just wouldn't come.
- I'm not sure who or how many, but thank you to all those who helped my mommy with the other things of life.
- Thank you, Luke, Zac, and Jacob for watching over me at night and keeping me safe when Mom and Dad went out.
- Thank you, Josh, for your extra attention and noticing so many of my needs.
- Thank you, Noah, for holding me so well and for your tenderness
- Thank you, Karis, for so many kisses and hugs.
- Thank you, Talyn, for being Mom's big helper, for becoming an expert at caring for my needs, and holding me so much
- Thank you all for your prayers and concern for me. From here I can see a huge mountain containing those prayers. Thank you for caring and helping me that way. Jesus has given me a glimpse of how the prayers protected me and saved my family from so much trouble. I can see now that your prayers brought me so much help at just the right time. I can now see how your love and concern for me encouraged my mommy and daddy.
- Thanks to everyone who held me. (John, Renee, Jim, Honey, Melissa, Sharon, Nancy, Lisa, Maggie, Joe, MaryAnn and many others). There were so many times I felt so out of control, but when you held me it felt so secure.

November 7, 2006 (Tuesday @ 1:49 pm)

It's been 3 days since Destiny has died. Yesterday – the funeral day – was the easiest as much as I feared that it would be the worst. It was encouraging to see so many people at the funeral and to hear their words of love and to see so many acts of kindness. Just as the memory of the standing ovation that we received at the baby dedication will always be so precious to us, so will the multitude of encouragement we received last night. It was overwhelming.

At this point, I can't imagine feeling happy again. Nothing satisfies – not eating, not watching a movie, not being around people, not shopping… All of those things are empty feeling – yet considering that they are just idols that I've used in the past to try to fill voids in my soul – why should I think that they would satisfy me now when the only thing that really satisfies is God? Those things bring temporary satisfaction; times like these reveal how empty those "fillers" are. I know that the time will once again come, unfortunately – when I will look for these things to fill an emptiness in my soul. May this time when none of these things satisfy remind me in the future to fill my hunger with God.

It's so easy for my mind to wander into the "what if" department. What if we didn't take her to the hospital. What if I would have been with her right before she died… What if I had fed more often the night we came home from the hospital? Then there's the "I wish" road that I

find myself going down. I wish that I would have kissed her more... I wish that we would have had more videos of her. I wish that I could remember what it felt like to hold her. I wish that I would have written more so that I could remember her better. These thoughts can easily send me into the pit of despair and sadness. The mind is such a powerful effector of the emotions. My mind needs to dwell on truth. God had her days numbered before the beginning of time. At the time of her death, I had no regrets. I did what I could do physically and emotionally throughout the short 3 months that I had her. I need to discipline my mind that I may not fall into self-pity.
Next random thought...

The last year has been filled with trial upon trial. My life was becoming defined by trial – a part of who I was. As much as I didn't want to be in a trial – I think that there was some sort of pleasure that I got out of it. There was an element of fame during our trials – everyone knew us and expressed their admiration of the way that we were walking through our trial. Because of the trial, I made allowances for myself to feel depressed and sad. People were willing to do absolutely anything for us. Although I didn't often take advantage of that, there was a sort of pleasure in our position. In the trial, as sad as it was, I always had a little bit of hope... maybe she would be able to do at least a little; maybe she would live a few years... maybe God would work a miracle. In the trial, I was constantly looking to see how God was going to use Destiny for a greater purpose. There was a lot of hope in that.

Now, although the trial isn't totally over – there's a lot of grief left – I'm feeling a sort of let down and emptiness. Who am I apart from this trial? What should I find pleasure in now? How do I redirect my significance? How am I going to rationalize my sadness or irritability? These questions have nothing to do with Destiny not being here and the sadness that I feel in missing her. These questions address some sin patterns that need to be dealt with – sin patterns that have always been there, yet have never been exposed. Again – I can see the loving hand God working his skillful scalpel.

Once again – the answer to these questions will come from a mind that is focused on truth rather than on emotions. There is a lot of hope right now. The end of the trial is not the end of my significance – it's the beginning of a new season where the lessons learned from the trial will propel us to be further used by God in a way we would never have been able to be used before. The trial stripped us of things that could have possibly been holding us back from being used by God in ways that we may have never dreamed of being used. We may serve in more obscurity – but we can be confident that God is still at work possibly in more powerful ways. May more glory be brought to Him and less to us. May I not find delight in the praise of man – but in the glorification of God. It's weird though – sometimes, the two cannot be separated. When we glorify God – it draws praise from men. May I not find significance in this praise – but be able to reflect it back to Him.

My focus needs to be on how I can serve, where I can be most effective, how I can do what God has called me to do better (like loving my husband and children and managing my home). I can't be looking for more things to fill my plate – it's a time to do what I already do better.

Beside Still Waters - Spurgeon
"Before I was Afflicted" Psalm 119:67
"The way to stronger faith usually lies along the rough path of sorrow."

I really want this cloud of sadness to pass. I want to grieve properly. My tendency is to go one way or the other – fall into deep sadness and cry a lot or compress all of my feelings in the name of faith. I'm trying to find a happy medium. I know that it is o.k. to mourn – yet I want to make sure that I'm mourning for the right thing. At times I feel like I'm mourning things that aren't worthy of mourning. So – to help me with my thought life, I'm going to write down all of the areas where my mind goes that makes me sad and then give myself truth to meditate on to give me a biblical perspective. Se here goes…

1. **The way that she died: I didn't get to hold her when she died; I could have prevented her dying by feeding her more.** Rebuttal: **Psalm 139:16 All the days ordained for me were written in your book before one of them came to be.** God had her death perfectly designed the way that He in His infinite wisdom deemed best. He knew what would have been best for me in her death. I did nothing wrong and in

wishing that I would have been holding her, I'm saying that God's ways aren't perfect – that my way would have been better. I need to trust God that she died when and where she did and not look back with regret.

2. **Time spent with her: I should have held her more her final days; I should have written more thoughts about her to help me to remember her more; I should have kept something with her smell on it.** Rebuttal: What happened cannot be undone, so there's no use in living in condemnation – it leads only to evil.

3. **My status has changed: I now only have 7 kids; I don't have a baby anymore; My youngest child is almost 5; we're not celebrities any more – just normal people.** Rebuttal: These thoughts are rooted in pride and must be repented of. My satisfaction in life should not come from fulfilling a desire to have the most kids, but in God who ultimately determines family size. At some point, everyone stops having babies. Yes, it's sad to not have a baby because the baby died instead of grew up, but I can't doubt God's hand in what I now have.

4. **How I feel: What am I going to do with my time? I miss holding her; I miss talking to her; I miss smelling her and stroking her hair; I just miss her!** Rebuttal: These are real feelings that to me seem worthy of being sad about. I can feel sad, but I shouldn't be paralyzed. I need to be grateful for the time I had with her while continuing to remember her and mourn for her. My sadness needs to be tempered with joy.

5. **The things I see: Seeing her clothes, stroller, car seat… make me sad; looking at pictures and videos; seeing one of her feeding gadgets…; when I see documents with her name on it; or mention of her death.** Rebuttal: This seems similar to point 6. These things are going to make me sad. But with each sad thought, there needs to be thoughts of

thankfulness, gratefulness, and joy. It could be an opportunity to pray that her life and death could be used for God's glory. That our family would be more useful for his kingdom; that salvation would result from her death.

Ps. 138:3 When I called, you answered me;
    you made me bold and stouthearted.

November 8, 2006 (Wednesday @ 3:07 pm)

I'm using this moment while I'm waiting to pick up the boys from football – to have my quiet time. All day today I have been reminded of the emptiness of idols; the only thing that truly and eternally satisfies is God. I can't imagine how I would be feeling right now if I attempted to find my comfort in the things of this world. The comfort would be fleeting at best. How does one who only used the things of this world for their satisfaction in life cope during a time like this? It's my relationship with the Lord that is truly sustaining me.

Isaiah 44
9 How foolish are those who manufacture idols.
    These prized objects are really worthless.
  The people who worship idols don't know this,
    so they are all put to shame.
10 Who but a fool would make his own god—
    an idol that cannot help him one bit?
11 All who worship idols will be disgraced
    along with all these craftsmen—mere humans—
    who claim they can make a god.
  They may all stand together,
    but they will stand in terror and shame.

Today is much better than yesterday. I can see that someday I will be able to laugh again without that heavy cloud looming over me. There was a lightness in my day today. There was no doubt that caring for Destiny was difficult both physically and emotionally. The weight feels lifted although I would have continued to bear the weight of her life gladly rather than have her die. I loved her so much. It seems like forever until I'll get to see her again – but in reality, it will be in a blink of the eye.

I keep thinking of what Joe read at the memorial service about a life's value is not in measured in years. I want to get a copy of that. My confidence in this trial has to be in a wise, loving and all-knowing God.

Beside Still Waters
THE FURNACE FOR GOLD – Prov. 17:3 - Spurgeon
"You had hoped for a miracle. My dear friend, sometimes God works a greater wonder when He sustains people in trouble than by delivering them. To let the bush burn with first and not be consumed is a greater thing than quenching the flame and saving the bush."

"When you come to your lowest point, God interposes. The tide turns when you reach the full ebb. The darkest part of the night is farthest from the rising of the sun. Believer, be of good courage."

November 9, 2006 (Thursday @ 2:52 pm)

I guess there is no way to make the pain go away sooner. COMPASS was kind of difficult today – seeing many people. My mind keeps going back to things like – Destiny was alive last week at this time… Now we only have 7 kids, not 8… I miss her… It took me 45 min. less to get ready for co-op today. I didn't realize how much extra work that she took. The work wasn't the hardest thing about Destiny – it was the emotions that were involved in the ups and downs of each day. The LORD was definitely merciful to me – though in His mercy there is still pain.

November 12, 2006 (Sunday @ 10:25 pm)

I had several thoughts today as I'm still in the reflecting and learning all that I can from my trial stage. I'll reflect on them more tomorrow – but so that I don't forget what I'm to reflect upon…

- If there is no obvious good from this trial – then it's still o.k. because God is still perfect in His plan. The trials good is not measured by the effect that it had on other people (such as salvation or encouragement.) My "duty" is to trust God even when I don't feel that there was any benefit in the trial.

- My significance cannot come from the acclamation that I get from walking through this trial well. I cannot get discouraged when the praise of me ends – which will happen. It is not about me – it's about glorifying God. When I get discouraged about being out of the limelight – it's because I'm a glory robber. My satisfaction needs to come from a desire to please Him alone.

- I got a glimpse today of what Christ went through on the road to the cross. In some way, I always thought that it wasn't too hard for Him because He was simply going to go to heaven as soon as He died. I kind of thought that He just needed to suck it up for the short period that He was on earth. However, even though the joy was set before me (I knew that there was good in the trial), it was (and is) painful. My hope was set on the joy, yet the pain is very real. His pain was very real as well. You don't want the pain; knowing that there is joy on the other side does help, yet no one wants to experience the pain.

Today I felt a definite lightness. It felt like I came out of a long lasting fog. It seemed to clear up very suddenly just like fog can immediately dissipate to find a bright shining sun. It almost feels like none of this last year happened. My deepest longing is for an 8th child. I think that I mourned the loss of Destiny before she was born and carried the fear of losing her the whole time that she was alive. I have so much confidence in the Lord's timing – knowing that her purpose on earth was complete.

As I was looking around at people in church today – I was again reminded that most everyone has a sort of trial going on in their life. Sometimes it doesn't matter how big the trial is because with God's grace proportioned to meet the trial – they can all feel just as weighty. May I remember the lessons that I learned (and am still learning) to apply to the continual trials (big and small) that I will face.

Finally – I remember Destiny and in a weird way honor her, by remembering the lesson that the Lord spoke to me in the last weeks of her life. I really feel like this may have been her main purpose… My responses to my children matter for eternity. Through her life, I feel like I've grown in patience and have a much different view of what is really important for me to do as a mother. Not to do, do, do – but to model godliness.

November 13, 2006 (Monday @ 7:40 pm)

Isaiah 41:10
...fear not, for I am with you; be not dismayed, for I am your God; I will strengthen you, I will help you, I will uphold you with my righteous right hand.

This is a good verse to meditate on often. It is true that He is with us and helping us through the trials that He designs for us. Though the road can be difficult – He is holding our hand.

How Firm a Foundation
By: John Rippon
How firm a foundation, O saints of the Lord,
Is laid for your faith in his excellent Word!
What more can he say than to you he has said
Who unto the Savior for refuge have fled?
Fear not, I am with you, oh, be not dismayed,
For I am your God and will still give you aid;
I'll strengthen you, help you, and cause you to stand,
Upheld by my righteous, omnipotent hand.
When through fiery trials your pathway will lie,
My grace, all sufficient, will be your supply.
The flames will not hurt you; I only design
Your dross to consume and your gold to refine.
Throughout all their lifetime my people will prove
My sovereign, eternal, unchangeable love;
And then when gray hairs will their temples adorn,
Like lambs they will still in my bosom be borne.

Beside Still Waters – p. 141
"This verse implies that your march through the flames will be quiet, calm, and safe. There is no need to increase your usual pace. If I had to go through literal fire, I would want to run and leap, but spiritually we are to walk through the fire."

It is true – we want to run through the fire (the trials) and get them over with quickly. Yet, God must desire us to walk through them – that all of the dross would be consumed.

I'm feeling a joy somewhere deep inside from the experience of walking through a fire and having my dross consumed. But even though I have a new type of joy, I would never choose to go through another type of trial. I can, however, look back and say that the trial was worth it (now that I can see it in retrospect). I don't think, however, that I would want to start it all over.

I don't think that I've written about God's mercy throughout our trial… Here are a few ways He was merciful:
- Destiny died on a Saturday when Jeff was at home.
- Her death was peaceful and at home – not in the hospital.
- She died before the holidays – when I would have been totally overwhelmed.
- The Lord knew my weariness, and though I didn't want her to ever die, He knew it was time.

- He taught me so many lessons from Destiny's life and one poignant one the week before she died that makes me feel was her purpose on earth.
- I have 7 other healthy children – she wasn't my first.
- God surrounded me with so many friends and tangibly showed us His love.
- He gave us the strength to glorify Him in the trial.
- Many non-Christians came to the funeral service.
- He's allowing me to see how He is merciful a week after her death.

November 14, 2006 (Tuesday @ 7:43 am) Jeff's Birthday
Isaiah 46:9 – 11
9 Remember the former things, those of long ago;
> I am God, and there is no other;
> I am God, and there is none like me.
10 I make known the end from the beginning,
> from ancient times, what is still to come.
> I say: My purpose will stand,
> and I will do all that I please.
11 From the east I summon a bird of prey;
> from a far-off land, a man to fulfill my purpose. What I have said,
that will I bring about; what I have planned, that will I do.

Beside Still Waters
"He guides the grain of dust in the March wind and the planets in their immeasurable pathways. He steers each drop of spray beaten back from the face of the rock. He leads the north star (Jer. 31:35). God is the dictator of destinies."

"Courage, dear friend. The Lord, the ever-merciful, has appointed every moment of sorrow and every pang of suffering. If He ordains the number ten, it can never rise to eleven, nor should you desire that it shrink to nine. The Lord's time is best. The span of your life is measured to a hair's width. Restless soul, God ordains all, so let the Lord have His way."

What will be will be. There is no sense fighting against what God has decreed since the beginning of time. It is much easier to surrender to the all-knowing, all-loving and all-wise God than to try to fight against his plan which He designed for our good and His glory.

Isaiah 48:10
> I have refined you, but not as silver is refined.
> Rather, I have refined you in the furnace of suffering.

Life feels pretty normal at this point. Last week I didn't think that the pain would ever subside. Now I'm dealing with my normal up and down feelings and have nothing to justify them with. I need to learn to speak to myself more about the truths that I know and not let myself fall into the pit.

November 20, 2006 (Monday @ 7:55 am)

All my resolve is wearing off with respect to how I respond to my children. "Destiny's Law" is fading – yet not forgotten. It's a goal that I continue to strive toward.

Yesterday during worship, I heard the Lord speak to me again. What I thought I heard Him say was, "Just as you walked in faith through the Destiny trial – you need to walk in faith with your other children. Entrust them to me. Finish this walk of faith well – just as you strove to finish the Destiny trial well. I am the same God who walked you through that – I will take care of the others." There was a wave of comfort that rolled over me and a new sense of hope for my children. I felt new courage to trust in God and not to fret. Once again, I don't know how long this "trial" is going to last – but I do know who I trust.

I read a good Spurgeon devotional today from the book Beside Still Waters; it fit with the theme of my life(?).

"God has not promised to rescue us according to our time schedule. If it appears that your prayers are unanswered, do not honor the Lord with unbelief. Waiting in faith is a high form of worship. In some respects, it excels the adoration of the shining ones above."

"God delivers His servants in ways that exercise their faith. He would not have them lacking in faith, for faith is the wealth of the heavenly life. He desires that the trial of faith continues until faith grows strong and comes to full assurance. The sycamore tree never ripens."

November 30, 2006 (Thursday @ 7:28 am)

I've felt absolutely miserable for the last week. Not only do I still have this terrible cough, emotionally I'm a wreck. I don't think that my emotions are from losing Destiny – but maybe they are some sort of whiplash. Who are Jeff and I apart from people caring for Destiny? Now that she's gone, I still can't get things done. Before I had her as an excuse – now I have to face myself – by myself. I thought that I'd be superwoman once I was no longer caring for her – but I can barely keep the necessary plates spinning let alone any extras. I'm short with the kids and mad at Jeff. What's going on here? How do I escape this misery?

Fenelon – Misunderstanding Prayer p. 88
"Return to prayer and inward fellowship with God no matter what the cost. You have withdrawn from God and now you find that God has withdrawn the sense of His presence from you. Return to Him and give Him everything without reservation. There will be no peace for you otherwise."

I guess that Fenelon gives the answer that I was looking for – I need to return to prayer and inward fellowship with God no matter what the cost. I've been coasting and now the "hill" won't take me any farther without some pedaling.

Lam. 3
20 I well remember them,
    and my soul is downcast within me.
21 Yet this I call to mind
    and therefore I have hope:
22 Because of the LORD's great love we are not consumed,
    for his compassions never fail.
23 They are new every morning;
    great is your faithfulness.
24 I say to myself, "The LORD is my portion;
    therefore I will wait for him."
25 The LORD is good to those whose hope is in him,
    to the one who seeks him;
26 it is good to wait quietly
    for the salvation of the LORD.

I think that Lamentations is a picture of sin's destructiveness. We think that we can play around with sin and it will not hurt us. Though these "terrors" happened physically to the Israelites, I can see them happening in a spiritual/emotional way to the people of our day.

When sin is not exposed, the problems multiply. This verse seems to be similar to our society as it seeks to deal with the symptoms of sin, rather than sin itself. It reminds me of psychologists who blame everything on the brain and cover up problems with medication. Sin can even look honorable at times – yet even so-called honorable sin – has consequences.

December

December 4, 2006 (Monday@ 7:24 am)

I've become so undisciplined! I can feel the effect of not being in the Word – my soul is becoming depressed. I'm out of the trial mode – yet I actually feel worse than when I was in the trial. Depression is crouching at my door. It's not as easy to cling to the promises of God. I'm not sure why. Now all is just blah – no aspiration of overcoming a trial by faith. Maybe someday I'll be able to figure out the difference – but for right now, I just need to press on and trust God to get me through this.

Fenelon – Inner Realities
"Live in the present moment. Tomorrow's grace is not given to you today. The present moment is the only place where you can touch the eternal realm."

Psalm 77
19 Your path led through the sea,
     your way through the mighty waters,
     though your footprints were not seen.
 20 You led your people like a flock
     by the hand of Moses and Aaron.

Psalm 78
34 Whenever God slew them, they would seek him;
     they eagerly turned to him again.
 35 They remembered that God was their Rock,
     that God Most High was their Redeemer.

I don't always want to have to be in a trial to draw near to God. Psalm 78 says that "whenever God slew them, they would seek him." My job right now is to honor God at all times. I'm not in the midst of a trial right now (though on the edge), but I can still draw near to God and seek to glorify Him in all that I do. I'm not as goalless as I feel – I need Christ even when it's seemingly smooth sailing. I'm just beginning to get a picture of purpose and reason for drawing near to God all day and purpose for my days without trial.

Joshua 1
6 "Be strong and courageous, because you will lead these people to inherit the land I swore to their forefathers to give them. 7 Be strong and very courageous. Be careful to obey all the law my servant Moses gave you; do not turn from it to the right or to the left, that you may be successful wherever you go. 8 Do not let this Book of the Law depart from your mouth; meditate on it day and night, so that you may be careful to do everything written in it. Then you will be prosperous and successful. 9 Have I not commanded you? Be strong and courageous. Do not be terrified; do not be discouraged, for the LORD your God will be with you wherever you go."

I feel the veil of depression lifting and am sensing new purpose in my life. The Word of God is truly living. Just one drink from its fountain is giving me the courage to continue. As Fenelon says – I need to live in the present moment – not looking to the fears of tomorrow. By faith, I need to glorify
God today – not worry about how I'm going to do that in the future. Yes, we are tight financially – but God has that under control, He knows what we need; yes, the house is overwhelming me – but God can give me the strength to get the work done; the kids aren't following the Lord wholeheartedly – but God is the One who brings life from death. I need to press on and entrust all things to God.

1 Peter 2
23 When they hurled their insults at him, he did not retaliate; when he suffered, he made no threats. Instead, he entrusted himself to him who judges justly.

December 11, 2006 (Monday @ 7:20 am)

Fenelon – Avoid Legalism pp. 98 - 99
"Learn not to exaggerate anything. Speak the truth without embellishment, but do not be hard with it. If you lean too much toward being exact, you will become legalistic."

"There is no use in always looking over your shoulder to see what has gone wrong. Press on to what is ahead with humility."

"Do not be afraid to lose sight of yourself and see Him alone."

I'm feeling really good these days. The depression left on Monday. It just seemed to have evaporated again - like fog on a summer morning. The last several nights lying in bed, I felt like I was the happiest – ever. It's odd how one's emotions can go up and down so sharply.

3 O Israel, put your hope in the LORD
   both now and forevermore.

December 12, 2006 (Tuesday @ 7:18 am)

Fenelon – Loved Ones p. 100
"You will never take care of your loved ones so well as when you are faithfully holding them up to God. You, as wise as you may seem, will only get in the way. Only that which comes from God can solve your difficult problems. You, of yourself, cannot convince anyone to turn to God."

Seems like what this whole devotional is saying is that the best way to love our family is to walk close to the Lord and receive wisdom from Him and to lift them up in prayer to Him who alone changes hearts.

Joshua 7
Sin makes us unproductive and hinders our battles. We need to purge sin from our lives and come clean before the Lord remembering His sacrifice for us on the cross for our sin.

Isaiah 53

He was oppressed, and he was afflicted, yet he opened not his mouth; like a lamb that is led to the slaughter, and like a sheep that before its shearers is silent, so he opened not his mouth. Yet it was the will of the LORD to crush Him; he has put him to grief…

December 25, 2006 (Monday @ 8 am)
Nancy Leigh DeMoss – Revive Our Hearts (Dec. 25, 2006)

"We need to learn to be content in mystery and say, 'Lord, if it pleases You in this moment to rescue me from this situation, I know that You can, and I   know that You will. And You may use angels as Your instruments to help   affect that deliverance. But if you don't, then I know that You have purposes that are greater than my immediate comfort and deliverance.'"

"Can you trust God to make the decision, to make the choice? Say, 'Lord, I leave it in Your hands.' And when the rescue comes, remember to look up and thank God and know that He well may have sent an angel as part of bringing that rescue about. "

Lam. 3:25 The LORD is good to those who wait for him, to the soul who seeks him.

Lam 3:37 Who has spoken and it came to pass, unless the Lord has commanded it?

January – Wrapping it up...

It's been over 2 months since Destiny has died. Every once in a while a memory of her will pop into my head, and I relive it. Then, at times I break down – feeling the loss of her precious life. Today I walked by a picture of her that I haven't seen in a while and the emotions welled up again. Besides those occasional periods of sadness, I feel thankful for what I went through in the last year. I'm glad that we had Destiny. I don't wish that it never happened. My heart's desire would have been for her to have been healthy and lived, yet I have full confidence that God knew better than I. She was a gift that He gave us for a time.

Her life and death have changed me in so many ways. My faith in God is so much deeper. Her life has helped me to see God at work in the "minor" trials of life. He feels more real to me, bigger, more loving, and wiser. My compassion towards others has increased since I can now relate to suffering a tad bit more. I desire to know this God who chose a perfect trial for me more. Who is this God who can bring such seeming adversity, sustain me through it as if I were being carried, give me joy and gratefulness after He removes my precious gift, and use her life to strengthen me in my inner being making me more effective for His Kingdom?

With all of our beings, we want to avoid suffering. We want to avoid pain and uncertainty (as I still do), yet how my view of suffering has changed. Suffering is not some random occurrence that we all experience at various points of our lives. I used to think that there was no real purpose in it – more of a punishment or test of sorts. Now, by God's grace, I can see trials as James says develops perseverance making us mature and complete. My joy has increased as I see what I faithful God I serve.

Resources:

The Seeking Heart - Francois Fenelon
All Things for Good - Thomas Watson
Trusting God - Jerry Bridges
God of All Comfort - Hannah Whitall Smith
Beside Still Waters - Charles Spurgeon

"Revive Our Hearts" radio broadcast with Nancy DeMoss Wolgemuth

June 2019